KU-200-716

CONTENTS

Introduction

CHAPTER 1   **A Blueprint for Success:**
Know Your Purpose 1

CHAPTER 2   **Why Have a Meeting:**
Is This the Best Way to Accomplish the Purpose? 7

CHAPTER 3   **Preparing Yourself:**
What, Who, When, Where and for How Long 13

CHAPTER 4   **Preparing Others:**
Letting Participants Know Your Expectations 23

CHAPTER 5   **Who's In Charge Here:**
Do's and Don'ts for Guiding the Meeting 27

CHAPTER 6   **Encouraging Participation:**
Wallflowers Have Ideas, Too 37

CHAPTER 7   **Handling the Tough Ones:**
Dealing with Difficult Situations 47

CHAPTER 8   **Collateral Materials:**
Reinforcement Rather Than Distraction 57

CHAPTER 9   **Audiovisual Assistance:**
Enhancement Rather than Clutter 63

CHAPTER 10 **Wrapping It Up:**
When Is Enough Enough? 69

CHAPTER 11 **Thumbs Up or Down:**
Assessing the Meeting 75

CHAPTER 12 **Writing it Up:**
Reporting the Results 81

**A Meeting Preparation Worksheet/
Checklist** 84

Index 87

BUSINESS SUCCESS GUIDES

Running a Meeting that Works

Robert F. Miller

A CASSELL BOOK

First published in the UK 1995
by Cassell
Wellington House
125 Strand
London
WC2R 0BB

Published by arrangement with Barron's Educational Series, Inc.,
Hauppauge, NY

Distributed in Australia
by Capricorn Link (Australia) Pty Ltd
2/13 Carrington Road
Castle Hill
NSW 2154

British Library Cataloguing in Publication Data
A catalogue record for this book is available from the British Library

ISBN 0-304-34559-8

Printed and bound in Great Britain by
Biddles Ltd, Guildford and King's Lynn

INTRODUCTION

One of the most famous—or perhaps infamous—meetings in all of English literature concludes with the stuffing of one participant into a teapot.

Probably that has not happened frequently in your experience, however often you've felt the urge. But it's not really stretching the point to compare the typical business meeting with the Mad Hatter's tea party in *Alice in Wonderland,* in which the seating arrangements are chaotic, the Mad Hatter speaks nonsense, the March Hare is rude, and the Dormouse sleeps through the proceedings. Nobody takes charge, the conversation goes in circles, and nothing is accomplished. Sound familiar?

Meetings can be one of the most productive tools of the work environment for stimulating ideas, fostering a sense of team spirit, generating plans of action, providing valuable guidance and, consequently, improving productivity. All too often, however, they are a complete waste of valuable time and energy. In 1989, *Industry Week* magazine estimated that $37 billion is wasted every year on poorly planned or poorly led meetings.

The purpose of this book is to provide you with a common sense approach to running a meeting that works. It offers a step-by-step process, starting with the decision to hold a meeting and ending with the final report on the proceedings. There are chapters on preparations for the meeting, taking charge, encouraging participation, handling difficult situations, using collateral materials and audiovisuals, and concluding and assessing a meeting.

This is a book about communication, about how people can come together with a shared purpose and accomplish their goals by talking with one another. It is about knowing what you want, organizing your thoughts, and articulating your ideas. It is about listening to and respecting the feelings and opinions of others. There are no clever gimmicks or mathematical formulas for success; running a meeting that works is as simple (which is not to say easy) as applying natural human communication skills to the work environment in a productive way.

What constitutes a meeting? There are conventions in faraway places, weekly staff meetings, and presentations aimed at landing a new account. There are "creative" sessions, bargaining sessions, and training sessions. There are sales and marketing meetings, press conferences, political meetings, and the annual meeting of the Order of the Garter. There are staff meetings and informational, problem-solving, and decision-making meetings. There are gatherings of three and assemblies of thousands.

It would be nice if this book were able to provide guidance in running all kinds of meetings, but its aim is less ambitious. This is a book about running the typical business meeting, the kind that takes place regularly in every office in America and that requires a leader to guide a small group of people through a communication process in a limited amount of time.

Whose idea is it to hold the meeting? The answer to that question has a major impact on the answers to many other questions raised in the following pages. Have you been asked to lead a meeting, or did you decide to hold it yourself? Whether it's deciding whom you should invite to participate, what the agenda should be, or what the meeting's goal is, much depends on who is calling the shots. Just how the advice in the next few chapters applies to your specific situation will depend on which decisions you are able to make. Bear this in mind as you read the book. We don't live in a perfect world, alas, and it may be impossible to keep the Mad Hatter away from your next meeting. This book will, however, provide some useful guidance no matter how your role as meeting leader has been defined or limited. At the very least, it will help you keep the Dormouse out of the teapot.

CHAPTER 1

A BLUEPRINT FOR SUCCESS:

Know Your Purpose

"Would you tell me, please, which way I ought to go from here?"
"That depends a good deal on where you want to get to," said the Cat.

—*Alice's Adventures in Wonderland*

"**W**hat are we doing here?"

How many times have you asked yourself that question while sitting through a meeting that seemed to have no direction? You glance at your watch, draw caricatures of the boss, and imagine your desk piling higher and higher with work that you must get done before the end of the day.

Studies of corporate work patterns indicate that some business executives spend as much as half their work lives in meetings of one kind or another. But how often are these meetings worth the preparation, time, and thought they demand of participants, as well as leaders? Isn't it true that most meeting participants, even those who really want to accomplish something, are convinced that the meeting will be disappointing? Why are most meetings so frustrating? The culprit, invariably, is a meeting leader without a sense of direction.

KNOW YOUR PURPOSE FOR MEETING

The first, and most important, step in running a meeting that works is knowing your purpose for calling the meeting.

The way you formulate your purpose in calling the meeting is critical in helping you organize your thoughts. Consider these examples.

"I've gathered you here today because we haven't had a meeting in a while." WRONG.

"I've gathered you here because I need to know what each of you is working on." RIGHT.

"The purpose of this meeting is to discuss the new product launch scheduled for tomorrow." WRONG.

"The purpose of this meeting is for me to tell you a few things about the product launch scheduled for tomorrow." RIGHT.

"We're here today because we've got to come up with some ideas for restructuring this department." WRONG.

"We're here today because I have some ideas about restructuring this department and I need your opinions on the subject." RIGHT.

A wise professor once said, "If you can't express your thoughts so that others can understand them, you don't know what your thoughts are." Know exactly what you hope to accomplish in the meeting and make that purpose clear from the outset; you should have clear in your mind the specific goal you hope to achieve.

It is not enough to want to discuss a subject; the discussion must have a focus. Do you want to discuss the subject of raises for everyone in the department because it's an interesting topic, or because you want to reach a decision about whether to raise salaries?

In formulating the purpose of the meeting it is often helpful to ask the question "Why?" Suppose the boss comes to you and says, "We need to have a meeting to talk about a new marketing plan." Ask why. What does he or she want to accomplish? Another example: Imagine you're put in charge of a project involving four other people. You think to yourself, "I'd better call a meeting." First, ask yourself why. What, specifically, do you want to accomplish?

DECIDING THE PURPOSE OF THE MEETING

The *purpose* of the meeting is not the same as the *subject* of the meeting. Suppose you call your staff together to plan the marketing strategy of a new product. The subject of the meeting is the new product;

the purpose of the meeting—what you hope to accomplish—is the exchange of ideas and information necessary to create a marketing plan.

In determining your purpose, it is often helpful to reduce it to its simplest terms. On the most basic level, there are only two basic purposes for any meeting—*to give information* or *to get information.* (Meetings may, of course, involve a combination of the two.)

Your first step in determining your purpose is to ask yourself, "Do I want to give information, get information, or both?" Your second step is to ask yourself, "What information do I want to give, get, or exchange?" For example, do you want a report from each attendee on his or her activities during the last week? Do you want to provide your staff with the schedule of events for tomorrow's product launch? Do you want input on your ideas for restructuring the department?

If you know exactly what you want to accomplish going into a meeting, chances are you'll have it coming out.

As you plan the meeting, bear in mind two words of caution: Be realistic. Can you accomplish your purpose? Do you have and understand the information you need to provide to others? Do they have the information you need? Do you have the time you need? Will the people you need to accomplish your purpose be at the meeting? Do you have the control or the decision-making power you need to accomplish your goal? Are you prepared for the meeting?

Many of these questions will be addressed in later chapters; all must be weighed as you decide on a realistic purpose for the meeting.

A meeting that works is a wondrous, exciting event. Sparks fly, gears shift, light bulbs flash on, and ideas bounce into receptive minds. Some meetings take a minute, others an hour or two; but it is always time well spent when the purpose of the meeting is understood, articulated, and accomplished.

CHAPTER 2

WHY HAVE A MEETING:

*Is This the
Best Way to
Accomplish
the Purpose?*

. . . it would have made a dreadfully ugly child: but it makes rather a handsome pig, I think.

—*Alice's Adventures in Wonderland*

Business communications come in many forms— memos, telephone calls, reports, faxes. Meetings are only one of many options. So before going any further, it might be wise to decide if having a meeting is the best way to accomplish your purpose.

WHY HAVE A MEETING?

The decision whether to have a meeting depends on a number of factors, such as the need you are attempting to satisfy. There are many possibilities:

- Do you need to pass along information or collect it from other people?
- Do you need to resolve an office conflict or a difference of opinion?
- Do you need a majority decision or evaluation on some issue?
- Do you want to generate a sense of team spirit?
- Do you want to be sure that the staff understands the nature of the next project?
- Do you want to provide training in the use of new equipment?

- Do you want to change a few people's minds on some issue?
- Do you need an immediate response to a problem?
- Do you want to convince a client to use your services?

Some of these needs can be best met in a meeting; others cannot. Most can be met in a number of ways, depending on your specific circumstances, talents, and work situation. Information, for example, can be provided in a meeting, memo, or report, depending on the nature of the information. An office conflict is best resolved by bringing the interested parties face to face privately. A majority decision can be obtained by a show of hands in a meeting, by correspondence, or telephone, depending on whether voters have advance access to the material being voted upon. Training can be accomplished via a manual or a meeting; much depends on the nature of the subject. A meeting may change some opinions, but so might one-to-one conversations. And a well-conceived, visually impressive written proposal may be just as effective in winning a client as a verbal presentation. For generating team spirit, however, a meeting can be one of the most effective tools.

To determine whether a meeting is the best tool for you to use, consider the following:

Cost

At first glance, the cost of gathering a few people in the conference room may not seem a big deal. A few simple calculations, however, reveal a different story. First of all, there are the salaries of the participants: the difference between the cost of an hour or two of your time alone and the cost of that time multiplied by the number of participants at their value per hour to the company can be significant. Then there is the cost to the company of your preparing for the meeting and the cost of any assistants helping you, as well as the cost of the time spent by other participants as they prepare for the meeting.

Take a meeting of ten people whose values per hour to the company are as follows: two supervisors at $100 per hour, three managers at $50 per hour, three account executives at $30 per hour, and two assistants at $15 per hour. A two-hour meeting of this group, not counting preparation time, costs the company $940.

Then there are the more tangible costs: materials, room rentals, refreshments, secretarial services, and possibly transportation. A recent "Meetings Market Report" by *Meetings & Conventions* magazine reveals that meeting planners spend 79 percent of their budgets on accommodations, transportation, and food and beverages. Your meeting may not require all these components; still, considering that a meeting planner's budget does not include cost to the company of participants' time, whatever costs you do incur may be significant.

Any kind of a meeting is expensive. In making your decision to hold a meeting, always compare its cost to the cost of alternatives. The only time cost does not matter is when there is no alternative to the meeting.

Restrictions

There is no point in scheduling a meeting if unavoidable restrictions make its success unlikely. Ask yourself the following questions:

- Do I have time to prepare for the meeting?
- Do other participants have the time to prepare themselves?
- Are all the necessary participants available and willing to attend?

If you cannot answer yes to all three questions, a meeting will be a waste of time.

The very nature of a meeting imposes certain restrictions on its effectiveness. Meetings are run, and attended, by human beings; put two or more humans in the same room and the chances for disagreement, confusion and inefficiency are great. After all, each of us is full of opinion, ideas, and emotions. Not every need is best met in a meeting. If you:

- have a simple message to deliver
- need a simple answer to a question
- have information to give that requires no immediate response
- don't have time to consider every side of the question or debate each issue
- are more persuasive or forceful on paper than in person

There may be more effective ways of accomplishing your purpose than having a meeting.

WHEN TO HAVE A MEETING

So how do you decide if a meeting is the best tool to use?

Assuming that the cost is not prohibitive, that there is time to prepare adequately, and that all the necessary players are available, a meeting is the right choice if:

1. **The interaction of opinions is necessary to create an idea, plan, or project.** Meetings are the way to go if a "creative" session in which the exchange of half-formed ideas leading to the generation of a fully formed concept is essential.
2. **Group dynamics are essential to the accomplishment of the purpose.** Meetings are valuable tools for generating team spirit at a sales meeting or staff meeting as you work toward a dynamic team presentation aimed at winning a new client.
3. **Time restrictions limit other options.** Meetings may be necessary in a situation in which group consensus is required but there is no time to circulate reports and wait for responses.
4. **The subject is sufficiently complex as to require interaction and explanation.** Meetings may be the best way to introduce a new product line or training staff to use a sophisticated piece of equipment.
5. **The boss says to hold a meeting.** Enough said.

A Bad (But Often Tempting) Reason to Hold a Meeting

The boss hands you a new assignment. "Double the company's profits—by tomorrow," you are instructed. You begin to organize your strategy. There are memos to write, assignments to make, information to gather and distribute. Overwhelmed, you say to yourself, "Maybe it would be easiest to have a meeting." Don't. All too often, a meeting seems to be the simple solution to a seemingly difficult situation. It *may be* the right solution, but don't hold a meeting simply because the alternatives seem daunting.

You may hate to write reports or memos. You may feel lost without colleagues with whom to try out new ideas. You may be afraid you can't handle an assignment alone. You might prefer not to do the research yourself. You may even want an excuse for having lunch at company expense or to escape the rest of your responsibilities. These are not reasons to have a meeting. Resist using meetings as an escape. Consider your options and put meetings to use where they are most effective.

CHAPTER 3

PREPARING YOURSELF:

*What, Who,
When, Where
and for
How Long*

"Begin at the beginning," the King said, very gravely, "and go on till you come to the end: then stop."

—*Alice's Adventures in Wonderland*

When you've decided what you want to accomplish at your meeting, you have taken the most important step in preparing yourself to be the meeting leader. From here on, it is a matter of organization.

Journalists are taught a basic rule of news reporting: tell who, what, when and where in as few words as possible at the top of the story. In preparing to lead a meeting, you can apply the same rule by asking yourself these questions:

- What kind of a meeting do I want?
- Whom should I invite?
- When should the meeting be scheduled?
- Where should I hold the meeting?

There's one other question you should answer: How long should the meeting last?

After you decide the purpose of your meeting and answer these questions, you'll be almost ready to take charge.

WHAT KIND OF MEETING DO I WANT?

There are two basic types of meetings: discussions and briefings. Discussion meetings are based on interaction:

Participants share ideas and opinions, contribute information, and possibly make decisions through some kind of voting process. Staff meetings, creative meetings, and problem-solving meetings are examples of interactive discussion meetings.

Briefings are meetings in which one or more speakers provide information to a group of listeners. There may be little group interaction apart from a few questions from the audience. News conferences, sales presentations, and training sessions are examples of briefings.

Of course, many meetings are a combination of briefing and group discussion. Your first task is to decide which type of meeting best suits your need. If your primary purpose is to communicate information to the group, perhaps a briefing is the most efficient way to go. On the other hand, if you need information from several people or there is a problem to solve or a plan to create, a discussion meeting is the likely choice.

WHOM DO I INVITE?

At a large public relations firm in New York, a certain kind of memo is circulated frequently. It says something like this: "We hope to pitch a new client, a theme amusement park in the Gobi Desert. There will be a creative meeting to discuss ways of promoting this product. Everyone is welcome; we need good ideas!" The memo is sent to dozens of executives, including those who promote everything from cameras and controversial drugs to candy bars and polyester clothing. The meeting date arrives; no one, other than the staff of the memo sender, shows up.

There is a simple but often difficult-to-follow rule for inviting people to a meeting:

Invite only those people who need to be there.

That means including only those individuals who have something specific to contribute, whether it is information or expertise. It may mean the people to whom you have information to give. A scatter-shot approach—"I guess I'll just throw this wide open and hope someone shows up with a valuable contribution"—is a waste of your time.

Invite only those people you are willing to listen to.

Have you ever tried to make a contribution in a meeting, only to find your ideas being dismissed or ignored by the leader? It happens all the time. This is not only rude to the individual concerned but unproductive, a waste of everyone's time. In determining your list of participants, invite only those people whose contributions you are willing to listen to and consider seriously.

"Why is Dracula in this meeting?" someone may ask. "You know, politics," is the invariable answer.

Do not use the protocol list to select meeting participants.

Admittedly, this is the most difficult rule to follow because office politics are an unfortunate part of the work environment, and it's often difficult to avoid inviting someone for no other reason than it's the political thing to do. Often, that person is The Boss.

But there's a good reason to try. Unless that person has another reason, such as expertise, for being in the meeting, a supervisor's presence can serve to distract participants from the subject under discussion and complicate the task of the leader who now has to run a meeting and "play politics" as well. In addition, from the perspective of the unneeded guest, the invitation may be considered an irritating obligation. Invitation by protocol can be a no-win situation for all concerned; the best advice is to try your best to avoid it.

HOW MANY PEOPLE SHOULD I INVITE TO THE MEETING?

The answer to this question depends on two factors: what kind of meeting it is and how many people *need* to be there. A study by the Center for Advanced Studies in

Behavioral Sciences in Palo Alto, California, found that the larger the group, the longer it took to make decisions; further, the study found that the decisions were identical to those made by smaller groups discussing the same topic.

If you are planning a group discussion, the general rule is the fewer participants, the better. Certainly there should be no more than a dozen. And it's often wise to take a page from Oriental philosophy and stick to odd numbers — three, five, seven, nine — particularly if decisions are to be made. An even number of participants tends to encourage "camps" or "sides" that can immobilize a meeting's progress; an uneven number of participants is more difficult to divide up.

For briefings, the number of participants is limited only by the size of the room and the strength of your voice. Whatever the type of meeting you have planned, the most important rule is to invite the people who need to be there.

A final note on the guest list: Invitations are just the first step. Participants also need to know what is expected of them in the meeting. This aspect of preparation is discussed in the next chapter.

WHEN SHOULD I HAVE THE MEETING?

It has been said that you should always buy a car that came off the assembly line on Tuesday, Wednesday or Thursday. Cars assembled on Monday are suspect because the workers are just back from a weekend and may be tired, distracted, or inattentive, while those that roll out on Friday may be victims of the T.G.I.F. syndrome. Similarly, teachers of small children try to do the "serious" stuff — English, social studies, math, science — in the morning, because by afternoon, attention spans are short. Perhaps meetings work by the same rules.

There are several simple guidelines to follow in deciding when to hold a meeting:

1. Allow Enough Time for Preparation. This means several things: time for you to invite participants and prepare your materials and presentation; time for participants to prepare what is expected of them; and time for the mailroom to prepare the handout materials for the meeting. Deadlines also must be considered; if the meeting's purpose is to prepare a report or presentation for a specific event, be sure you allow time to have the meeting and then do the necessary follow-up work before the deadline. Don't get caught finishing the work after the party's over.

In timing your meeting, work backward from the deadline — "The report is due at the end of the month. We need one week to prepare documents *after* the meeting. I'll have to review those documents. That will take three days, and the staff needs a week to prepare *for* the meeting, so I'd better schedule it for . . ."

2. Schedule Meetings on a Date When All Necessary Players Are Available. It makes sense to confirm attendance in advance of setting the final date.

3. Avoid Scheduling a Meeting on Holidays, Long Weekends, and at the Beginning or End of the Week. This may seem obvious, but a quick glance at the calendar is always a good idea.

4. Morning Meetings Are More Productive Than Those Scheduled Late in the Day. Our attention spans may be slightly longer than those of children, but there is a tendency to become more and more enmeshed in work as the day proceeds. Late in the day, meeting participants may be distracted by other tasks and therefore less forthcoming in their contributions. They may also feel some resentment at having to drop what they are doing to attend a meeting.

5. Don't Mix Business with Pleasure. Attempts to combine a meeting with lunch, dinner, or a reception often meet with disappointment. Attention to the serious matters at hand is diluted, particularly at dinner or reception meetings. There's nothing wrong with socializing; just don't try to do business at the same time.

If you must schedule a meeting at a mealtime, try breakfast. Breakfast meetings tend to be well-attended (because you catch people before their work day starts), short, and productive.

If you must have a meeting with lunch, dinner, or drinks, be sure to use adjoining rooms—one for the meeting, the other for socializing. The meeting *always* should come first. And avoid the pitfall of scheduling business between courses of a meal, unless you don't care that no one is listening. Such a schedule is *always* a mistake.

WHERE SHOULD I HOLD THE MEETING?

A press briefing took place recently in an elegant restaurant in New York at breakfast time, when the restaurant was closed to other patrons. The service was excellent, the food superb, and the setting magnificent. The invited guests were clustered in close proximity to the speaker, who rose to thank them all for coming out so early in the day. He went on to discuss his company's exciting new services. The only problem was the lovely waterfall that made the setting so magnificent—it completely drowned out his words.

The choice of location for a meeting depends on several factors, including the presence or absence of waterfalls. Of course, you may have little choice in the matter, but, assuming you can select a location, keep in mind the following considerations:

1. Make the Location Convenient. Be sure that the location is accessible to all participants—that is, within easy reach of their respective offices.

2. Pick a Neutral Spot. If the purpose of your meeting is to resolve conflicts or solve a problem, it may be best to pick a neutral corner—a location that gives no advantage to any group or individual.

3. Be Sensitive to Politics. Some meetings require a sensitivity to politics. If you're making a presentation to a prospective client, for example, it is wise to go to the client's office rather than ask the client to come to yours. If The Boss is an essential participant in your meeting and his office is on the thirty-fourth floor, it may be expedient to hold the meeting in his conference room rather than yours.

4. Check the Cost. Be sure the location of your choice can be accommodated in your meeting's budget.

5. Pick the Right Facilities. This consideration may be the most important of all. Does your location have the appropriate seating for your type of meeting? Does it offer the right level of comfort? (First class may be all right for airlines, but too plush a setting may serve as a distraction.) Do you have access to whatever audiovisual equipment you require? Are there catering facilities suitable to your needs? Is there access for the handicapped?

HOW LONG SHOULD THE MEETING LAST?

A meeting should last as long as it takes to accomplish its purpose. The secret, of course, is having a realistic purpose. There are no hard-and-fast rules about the length of meetings; some are over in minutes, while others drag on for hours. Certainly, no meeting session should last more than one hour without a break of ten minutes or more.

You should remember that you're dealing with people, not machines. Attention spans vary, and even the most interesting subjects in the world pall after being discussed for more than an hour or two at any one time. Can you honestly expect people to stay interested in marketing plans or staff reports for any longer? If your session lasts more than two hours, your purpose is too ambitious for one meeting. The meeting's productivity is likely to be less than cost-effective, and you should consider scheduling two or more sessions.

PREPARING FOR THE MEETING

Having asked *what, who, when, where* and *how long*, you face only one more task in preparing for a meeting: doing the work you need to do in order to be well-informed.

Good intentions on the part of a meeting leader mean little if he or she enters the meeting unprepared. You know the purpose of the meeting and what you want to accomplish. You've decided whom to invite, when and where to hold the meeting, and what to expect from the participants. Now you need to determine what you expect from yourself. As a final step in preparing yourself to lead the meeting with confidence, ask the following questions:

- What information do I need in order to lead this meeting?
- Is that information readily available? Where can I get it?
- Do I need to prepare any written materials?
- How long will it take me to prepare myself?
- Do I need assistance in preparing for the meeting?

Then do the work.

Note: At the end of this book is a checklist you can use as a guide in preparing yourself and others for a meeting.

CHAPTER 4

PREPARING OTHERS:

*Letting Participants
Know Your
Expectations*

"The time has come," the Walrus said, "to talk of many things."

—*Alice's Adventures in Wonderland*

The phone rings. It's the boss's assistant, who says, "There's been a meeting scheduled to develop next year's marketing plan." "Fine," you respond, "when is it?" "In five minutes," she says. Incredible but true; it happens all the time.

No matter how carefully you prepare to lead a meeting, your efforts will be for naught if you fail to prepare the other participants adequately as well. It's to your advantage to have well-prepared participants. Giving them enough time to do the research, prepare the report, check the files, or give some thought to the subject of the meeting is just one part of helping them to be ready.

PROVIDING THE NECESSARY INFORMATION

Essential to preparing the participants of a meeting is providing them with the information they need in order to make a valuable contribution.

1. Tell Them the Purpose of the Meeting As Well As the Subject. "We are meeting to formulate a marketing plan for the Imperial Widget Company." Or, "There will be a staff meeting in order to outline the status of all current projects."

2. If More than One Subject Is to Be Discussed, Be Sure to Outline the Agenda of the Meeting. There should be no surprises; a subject introduced without warning will be the subject of a fruitless discussion. All participants deserve the courtesy of knowing in advance all the topics to be raised in the meeting.

3. Tell Them What Is Expected of Them. "Please be prepared to offer several ideas about how we might market Imperial Widgets." Or, "Please be prepared to report on the status of your projects." In some cases you can prepare a blanket directive to all participants; in other cases, you may need to make requests to individual attendees. Be specific in requesting the information you need.

4. Tell Them When and Where the Meeting Will Be Held and How Long You Expect It to Last.

There are three things you should remember when providing the information meeting participants need to prepare themselves:

1. Allow Plenty of Time for Preparation. Take into consideration what you expect of those invited to the meeting; give them time to prepare the report or to review their work. Above all, give them time to think about the purpose of the meeting and its subject.

The more you expect from meeting participants, the more time they should have to prepare.

2. Put It All in Writing. Do not give instructions or describe expectations over the telephone, because you can never be sure that you have the full attention of the listener. At the moment of your call he or she might be deep in thought about something else, on another call, or spilling coffee. Whatever you do, don't rely on phone-mail or fax messages.

3. Confirm that All Participants Have Received the Message. You or your assistant should confirm by telephone

that your outline containing the purpose, agenda, and particulars of the meeting has been received and understood: "Hi, George. Did you get my memo about the meeting? Can you make it? Do you understand what I need from you? Great, see you next Thursday at 10 A.M."

A well-prepared participant is a productive participant. Do everything you can to make it possible for attendees to contribute productively to the meeting.

CHAPTER 5

WHO'S IN CHARGE HERE:

*Do's and Don'ts
for Guiding
the Meeting*

The players all played at once, without waiting for turns, quarrelling all the while . . . and in a very short time the Queen was in a furious passion, and went stamping about, and shouting, "Off with his head!"

—*Alice's Adventures in Wonderland*

This staff meeting actually took place:

Summoned for a 10 A.M. meeting, the staff assembled in a conference room and waited for The Boss. As minutes ticked by, various individuals drifted in and out of the room, fixed coffee, and chatted in the corners. At 10:15 The Boss arrived with a load of papers and, without a "Hello" or "Sorry I'm late," said, "We've got a lot of work to do."

Calling on one staff member for a progress report, The Boss began rustling through papers and searching through folders. Minutes later he left the room without warning, leaving the speaker in midsentence. A few minutes later, The Boss was back. "Go on," he said; as the speaker tried to pick up where she had left off, The Boss turned to his assistant and began a whispered conversation. Then he was across the room talking on the telephone, then back to his papers, then gone once more without warning. At no time did the leader of the meeting sit still, look a participant in the eye, and listen to a conversation. After more than an hour of reports and attempted discussions—all of which were constantly interrupted, broken off, or ignored—the leader concluded the meeting by saying, "I'm just not getting enough work out of you; I have to do everything myself."

This is a case of a meeting without a leader, despite the presence of someone ostensibly making the rules—an exercise in futility. Needless to say, the only accomplishments were exasperation and bruised feelings on the part of the staff and frustration on the part of The Boss. An extreme case, perhaps, but typical of how far too many meetings are run in offices throughout America, according to interviews with executives and meeting participants in offices across the country.

Running a meeting that works is really not very difficult. Essentially it requires two things of the leader:

Maintaining control over the proceedings and giving the meeting his or her undivided attention.

George David Kieffer, author of *The Strategy of Meetings* (Simon & Schuster, 1989), argues that too many meetings tend to end in "collective incompetence"; he defines the "winning" meeting as one in which the leader takes charge and takes responsibility for the proceedings. Here are some suggestions that will make taking charge easier:

Do Your Homework. Come to the meeting prepared, having done the research, prepared the reports, or reviewed whatever material is to be discussed. Know the purpose of the meeting.

Remember the Process. Every meeting has four steps: *presenting the information, evaluating the information, coming to a decision, and taking action.* An understanding of these steps should underlie everything you do to lead a meeting. The substance of each step, of course, varies depending on your goal for the meeting; nevertheless, the four steps can be applied to virtually every kind of meeting.

Step 1, presenting the information, includes presenting the purpose of the meeting and the facts or ideas necessary to achieve the purpose: "Today we need to develop a plan to expand our sales force. I'd like each of you to offer some ideas on how to do that."

Step 2, evaluating the information, is the discussion phase in which all participants debate the merits of the ideas or facts already presented.

Step 3, coming to a decision, is the process of resolving the problem: "We are agreed, then, that the best way to expand the sales force would be to . . . Is that correct?"

Step 4, taking action, is the implementation of the decision. This stage begins with making assignments in the meeting and ends with following up on the actions decided on. In our example, this might mean asking one group of people to draft a final report on the sales-force expansion, asking another person to discuss the matter with the personnel department, and asking yet another to meet with the accounting department. A timetable for completion of these tasks should be agreed upon before you adjourn the meeting. Then it's up to you to follow up in the weeks to come.

Distribute an Agenda. The agenda should be distributed to all participants at the beginning of the meeting and should include the purpose of the meeting, a list of all topics to be covered, and an approximate amount of time for the discussion of each subject. Be sure that subjects are listed in the order in which you wish to discuss them. The agenda should be brief, so that it can be easily and quickly read, but detailed enough so that participants understand what you mean by the purpose of the meeting as well as each topic to be discussed.

Consider Your Seating Plan Carefully. Seating can play an important role in shaping the tone as well as the substance of a meeting. In *Essentials of Nonverbal Communication,* Mark Knapp argues that seating behavior is not random and that how people seat themselves has an impact on how the meeting proceeds. He also claims that communication tends to go back and forth between people rather than around a table.

If you want participants to sit quietly and listen, it might be wise to arrange chairs in a classroom configuration. If you want to encourage discussion and generate a sense of team spirit, use a round table with no obvious sides. A rectangular table tends to encourage dominant personalities to take charge by sitting on the ends or in the middle of one side, often the side with the fewest seats, Knapp maintains. It's also interesting to note that, according to research, placing naturally shy or nondominant personalities in positions of dominance—at the end of a table, for example—does not make them participate more.

A meeting should be neither a social event nor a battleground. Seat your participants in such a way that neither business alliances nor social cliques are reinforced. If this is a problem-solving meeting, avoid seating factions across a table from each other; on the other hand, if you want to present a strong united front to a client or competitor, group your forces facing the other participants. If anyone is to make a presentation, be sure that person is clearly visible and easily heard from his or her position.

Introduce the Participants. In a discussion meeting, be sure that the names, positions, and areas of expertise of each participant are announced at the beginning of the meeting, either by you or by having each individual introduce himself or herself. This is more than common courtesy; it ensures that no participant is placed at a political disadvantage.

Establish the Rules. If this meeting is to be governed by rules—company regulations, Robert's Rules of Order, your own rules—announce them at the outset and be sure that everyone understands them.

Get All the Facts or Ideas on the Table Before Evaluating Them. It makes sense to introduce all the information before discussing or debating its merits. For example, if the purpose of the meeting is to generate a plan of action for the next quarter, ask for ideas without discussion until all ideas have been offered. Then debate the merits of each proposal. This approach both encourages people to volunteer ideas and prevents the meeting from bogging down in a discussion of the first proposal.

If background information or expertise is necessary to move the discussion along, it is the leader's responsibility to provide it. For example, if the discussion of a new computer software program requires knowledge of other comparable systems, it's up to you to provide that information or know who else in the room has it and call on that person for the information.

Keep the Ball Rolling. It is up to you to keep the meeting moving forward. This can be done in a number of ways:

1. Keep an eye on the clock. Stick to the time allotted in the agenda to each item of discussion. Remember, a meeting is not necessarily democratic. You're the boss, and it's enough to say politely, "It's time we moved on; if we have time we'll return to this subject later."

2. Know your questions in advance. Part of your preparation for the meeting should be a list of questions to which you need answers. Knowing them in advance prevents your forgetting them in the course of the meeting.

3. Keep the conversation relevant. This is probably the single hardest task of a meeting leader and, in the interests of productivity, the most important. Again, remember that a meeting is not a democracy; on matters of running the meeting, no one gets to vote but you. Whenever a participant strays from the subject, a reminder is in order. Perhaps the question "Could you relate what you've just said to this particular situation?" will do the trick. Or a gentle "In the interests of time, I think we'd better get back to the subject at hand" may suffice.

4. Summarize the proceedings as you go. As leader, it's up to you to provide a summary of the discussion at regular intervals, preferably when switching from one subject to another. This both helps participants organize their thoughts and keeps the discussion within a manageable framework.

Insist on Conclusions and Action. At the end of the meeting, be sure that participants have arrived at a consensus of opinion. That consensus should include decisions made and actions to be taken. Summarize the group's conclusions, focusing on any actions decided upon. "It is my understanding that we have agreed that a new sales strategy is essential and that, in the next three weeks, each of you will draft an element of the plan as it pertains to your department. Is that how all of you see it?"

Be sure to review whatever assignments were given in the course of the meeting so that participants leave the room knowing exactly what their next step is.

Communicate with Class. Your communication skills help set the tone for the entire meeting, and your ability to express yourself well and to encourage others to do the same helps make the difference between a productive and an unproductive meeting.

Some pointers:

1. Help others to express themselves well. You can do this by asking for clarification when it's needed: "I understand you to mean . . . Have I got it right?" or by asking for a summary: "Could you summarize that point for me? I'm not sure I understand." In encouraging others to express themselves, be certain not to criticize their efforts. Saying "You don't make any sense; could you repeat that?" does little except embarrass the victim and encourage silence.

2. Avoid editorializing. As meeting leader, you are certainly entitled to your opinions. In the interest of generating a lively discussion in which all participants feel comfortable about expressing theirs, however, it is essential that you clearly label your opinions as such: "My opinion on that matter is . . ." Otherwise, make every effort to keep your opinions out of the discussion. Phrase your questions, for example, in a neutral way. There's a world of difference between "Don't you think that idea is rather weak?" and "What do you think about the merits of that idea?"

3. Offer your colleagues the same courtesies you expect from them. Rudeness, aside from bruising the feelings and often denting the self-esteem of others, is unproductive. If you want the most out of your meeting participants, treat them nicely! Look them in the eye when talking to them; don't talk when they are talking; don't leave the room for any reason without declaring a break in the meeting; don't do other work while the meeting is in progress; and hold all telephone calls.

Keep the Discussion Balanced. As meeting leader, you face the task of seeing both sides, or as many sides as are presented, of the story. Whereas other participants may have a position to present or defend, your role in mediating the discussion is to balance the ideas and opinions. You can do this most effectively by recognizing one opinion and asking for others: "I understand what you're saying, George. Does anyone have a different approach?" *In order to make the most informed decision, it is best to consider as many viewpoints as possible.*

Break Up the Fights. Healthy disagreement is one thing; fighting is another. It is your responsibility to maintain order in a meeting by insisting that all players stick to the rules and the subject under discussion. Any personal attacks must be stopped *immediately.*

Listen, Listen, Listen.

> *You go up to the counter of a fast-food chain and wait to get the attention of the teenager behind the register, who is chatting with his burger-flipping*

buddy. Finally he faces you and you say, "I'd like a double cheeseburger, small order of fries, and a small Coke." "Do you want fries with that?" he replies. "Yes," you say, "that's what I said." "What size drink do you want?" he asks.

We are, alas, a nation of nonlisteners. The loss in revenues, profits, and productivity to businesses resulting from poor listening habits totals $1 billion a year, according to Dr. Lyman Steil, formerly a professor of rhetoric at the University of Minnesota. Dr. Steil is quoted in *American Salesman* magazine as saying that 80 percent of waking hours are involved in communication, only 45 percent of that time listening.

Your ability and willingness to listen is essential; they make the difference between a meeting that is efficiently conducted and that produces well-thought-out ideas and opinions and one that is not cost-effective and that is marked by inconclusive results. So how do you learn to listen?

In the theater, actors are often given a "side," a card containing their lines but not the other actors', only the cue words signaling when it is time for the actor in question to speak. The result? The actor has to listen, because he or she has no idea when the cue will come or what the gist of the conversation preceding it is. The result, on stage, can be a heightened sense of natural conversation rather than of actors reciting memorized lines.

In the course of a meeting, participants, too, have no idea what others will say next. Unfortunately, we tend to be preoccupied with what *we* plan to say next, particularly since we naturally want to look and sound our best. As meeting leader, you should make every effort to ask questions because you want to *hear* the answers. Train yourself to listen, assimilate what was said, and *then* respond. Have questions prepared in advance so you don't have to think of them while someone else is speaking. Practice will help you direct the flow of conversation easily, keep the discussion relevant, and provide a valuable framework of give-and-take within which other participants can work together to accomplish your goal.

Keep the Record Straight. One of the simplest, and most often forgotten, steps in running a successful meeting is taking notes. Be sure that someone other than you, preferably someone with legible handwriting or a laptop computer, records the proceedings of your meeting. The minutes should detail, in outline form, all subjects discussed, any decisions reached, and relevant opinions and ideas offered during the discussion, including the participant who offered the idea. In choosing someone to take notes, it is advisable to pick someone who has no ax to grind—that is, someone who will record the proceedings without bias and without giving more or less weight to specific opinions, ideas, or decisions than they deserve.

CHAPTER 6

ENCOURAGING PARTICIPATION:

*Wallflowers Have
Ideas, Too*

"Give your evidence," the King repeated angrily, "or I'll have you executed whether you are nervous or not."

—*Alice's Adventures in Wonderland*

Participation is the very soul of a meeting. There are, of course, briefings in which speeches by one or more individuals dominate the proceedings, but rarely is there a meeting of any kind that does not involve some give-and-take, some interaction of ideas and opinions.

A meeting that works is one in which all participants can express their thoughts without fear of ridicule or reprisal, secure in the knowledge that their contributions will be heard and taken seriously, if not always agreed with. Such an environment allows the most productive ideas to rise to the top, the result of a creative process involving conversation, disagreement, and, finally, consensus. You face no greater challenge in your role as meeting leader than to create this kind of atmosphere.

Much of the quality of the interaction in a meeting depends on you. It is your job to coax ideas from each participant, stimulate discussion, and guide the group to the decision-making stage (if that is the purpose of the meeting). Whether you succeed depends on two factors: the meeting environment you create and your skill at getting the most from your participants.

CREATING AN ATMOSPHERE FOR PARTICIPATION

Each of us is profoundly affected by the world around us, specifically by the people around us. Walk into a room full of angry people and you feel the tension; join a group celebrating a happy occasion and you feel the excitement. Take part in group meditation and you're apt to feel the serenity of the moment.

The same applies to the work environment. The Boss is tense and harried; you become tense and worried. The sales figures are up; everyone relaxes. Much of the quality of discussion and debate in your meeting depends on the energy and the personality you bring to it. If you arrive angry, tense, determined to prove a point, or suspicious, you're likely to have a roomful of mummies to contend with. On the other hand, if your mood is relaxed, friendly, and unhurried, you are likely to have a roomful of talkers. It's up to you to set the tone of the meeting. These are some ways to go about it:

1. Join the Meeting With an Open Mind

Leave your preconceptions and assumptions behind and enter the meeting with a desire to learn, to find out, to hear what's happening.

2. Start Off with a Smile and a Greeting

You wouldn't think of meeting a group of friends without at least a "Hello!" Why should a meeting be any different?

3. Respect the Differences Among People and Work With Them

Like it or not, people's personalities differ: Some are loud and boisterous, others quiet as mice. Not everyone is easy to work with. But it's a lot easier to work *with* the differences than to try to change them to make yourself comfortable. Be prepared to accept those you find difficult, encourage those who are timid, and keep a healthy perspective with your friends. The ideal meeting is one in which everybody takes part; how well you accept the many personalities in the room helps determine how many are willing to play the game.

4. Recognize Individual Expertise and Talent

No one likes to be one of the herd, so give individuals a chance to shine. In the course of discussions, call on those you know have something of value to contribute. If there are a number of strangers in the crowd, it might be wise to ask, "Does anyone else here have some expertise or ideas on this subject?"

5. Give Credit and Thanks Where They Are Due

Nothing is more disheartening, particularly for junior members of the company, than to have their ideas and opinions appropriated by someone else. And it happens all the time. Rob the Rookie presents an idea to Sam the Supervisor, and by the time it gets to Grinch the Boss the idea has become Sam's. In many cases the switch is unintentional; in others it's deliberate. You can foster a sense of security and confidence in a meeting by being sure to acknowledge to the group your awareness and appreciation of someone's idea: "That's an interesting idea, Rob; I like the way you think. Does anyone else have a comment on Rob's idea?"

6. Accept the Challenge of Others

As leader, you are in the hot seat. It's your responsibility to accept criticism of your ideas, even of the way you run the meeting, as long as the criticism is directed at your actions or opinions rather than at your person. If someone says, "You're a damned fool," a sharp rebuke is called for. But if the challenge is directed at your ideas, it's up to you to respond without getting defensive.

7. Be Sincere

Have you ever noticed how people have different personalities for the different roles they play? The change often
happens when they're asked to take on new responsibilities. A colleague with whom you've joked and eaten chili
dogs on the street gets promoted and suddenly starts
wearing vests and talking in a deeper voice. Now he eats
sushi, in restaurants. "I thought I knew that guy. Suddenly
he's a different person," you think to yourself. When you
run a meeting, be yourself. After all, you're in a room with
people who have the same kind of worries and fears that
you have. The disguise takes too much energy, and in the
end it won't fit right anyway. Let yourself show through;
it's the best way to establish a productive working
relationship.

8. Respond to Signals

Take the pulse of your meeting by responding to verbal
and nonverbal signals that tell you what the participants
are experiencing. In a back issue of *Meetings & Conventions*, Carl Camden, of Cleveland State University's
Department of Communications, offers a checklist of signals and what they mean. Fidgeting and wandering eyes,
for example, signal inattention; to counter such signals,
you might ask questions or ask a participant to speak.
Avoiding eye contact or raising voice pitch may mean the
group members are anxious. Camden suggests you ask
them directly what's troubling them. When discussions are
nonproductive, the group is likely to take on a defensive
posture, making negative and exaggerated comments such
as "That's dumb," or "You always do that." You can get
things back on track by asking the most vocal participants
to argue the other side or to listen to others without
speaking for a few minutes, Camden says.

NOW SOME "DON'TS":

1. Don't Dominate the Discussion

As much as you'd like to set the world straight on a few things, this is not the time to do so. Your role is to moderate the conversation, making sure everyone has equal time. A few ideas, an opinion or two, particularly when laying the groundwork for the discussion, are perfectly acceptable. Otherwise, bite your tongue and ask the questions.

2. Don't Harass the Witness

You may have the authority to make the meeting rules, but you don't have the power to change people's opinions (however wrong you know they are) or change personalities. You can't badger someone into offering an opinion, and you shouldn't humiliate someone into holding his tongue.

3. Don't Interrupt (With Exceptions)

"Do unto others as you would have them do unto you" holds true in running a meeting. Politeness goes a long way in accomplishing your task of encouraging everyone to participate. An interruption, except in the case of a particularly long-winded speaker who lost sight of the subject minutes ago, is an unnecessary insult.

4. Don't Get Personal

However strongly you disagree with someone, no matter how exasperated you are at someone's behavior, ad hominem attacks are unproductive. There are better ways of encouraging a wallflower to speak than by saying, "I know you're real shy, but don't you have something offer?" It's desirable to accept the wide range of personalities in the room but quite unacceptable to bring those personalities into the conversation.

5. Don't Insist on Participation Simply for the Sake of Participation

It would be nice if everyone felt comfortable speaking in front of others, but the fact is not everyone does. If, after gentle prodding, a member of the group is still obviously happier as a silent partner, don't push. Offer that person, and all the others, the opportunity to communicate any thoughts to you in private or on paper. At the end of the meeting you might say, "I'll be available in my office if anyone wants to discuss any of this further. Or jot down your thoughts and drop them off when you have the chance. But don't waste time, we have to move on this in a hurry."

6. Don't Embarrass Yourself with Bad Humor

A sense of humor is a terribly personal thing; one person's joke is another person's insult. There's certainly room for good humor, but a meeting is rarely a place for jokes. If you want your audience to have a laugh, make yourself the object: "A funny thing happened to me on the way to this meeting . . ."

GETTING THE MOST FROM THE GROUP

Creating the right atmosphere for participation in a meeting is more than half the battle; people who feel comfortable and secure will *want* to share their thoughts or opinions. There are, however, a number of ways you can build on that success to maximize the quality of the group's interaction.

1. Act As If You *Expect* Everyone to Participate

From the outset, let it be known (by making eye contact, smiling, keeping your comments brief, asking questions) that this meeting is for discussion, not speeches.

2. Ask the Right Questions

The goal of questioning in a meeting should be to get people to talk, to elaborate, to explain, or to theorize; in other words, to feel comfortable about expressing themselves fully and honestly. Structuring your questions in the right way can help. Never ask a question that requires only a "yes" or "no" unless all you want is a vote. Ask for opinions and speculations; ask difficult questions based on the group's expertise. Don't sound condescending or hostile. Be sure your questions are clearly phrased and easily understood; they should be short and to the point.

3. Look For Opportunities to Include As Many People As Possible in the Discussion

Let it be known that contrasting opinions are welcome. As one person finishes a comment, turn to the group and ask, "Does anyone else have an idea on that?"

4. Take Every Opportunity to Expand the Subject

One useful method of drawing new speakers into the discussion is by stretching the subject to include new thoughts and facts through remarks such as, "That's very interesting. I wonder if we could carry it further or apply it in other ways. Does anyone else care to comment on that?" or, "I like that idea. Do you think we could apply it to the idea we were discussing a minute ago?"

5. Use the Group's Expertise and Talents to Increase Participation

It's always nice to be recognized for having a skill or knowledge, and a smart leader knows that acknowledging an individual's expertise is a good way to draw that person into a discussion: "George, I understand you've done some work in this field. Are we on the right track here? What's your opinion?"

A WORD ABOUT CONFLICT

One of the most difficult aspects of human interaction is learning to disagree without fighting. Conflicting opinions, for most of us, all too quickly become "conflict." In family life, the disagreement may escalate to flying pots and pans. In office life, for the most part, the anger triggered by a difference of opinion festers as resentment and suspicion. To avoid such difficult situations, many of us sometimes go to unnecessary extremes to avoid any sign of disagreement.

Conflict is okay. While you may hope it doesn't occur, you should not be afraid of it. No one said that everything about a meeting has to be cheerful. Strong disagreement is bound to generate a few emotions. It can generate some sound thinking as well—but only in a controlled environment. It's up to you as meeting leader to maintain that control.

The best way to maintain control is by insisting that all parties stick to the subject at hand and refrain from personal remarks. By restricting the boundaries of disagreement to one subject, you force participants to leave the larger, emotion-packed issues—the hidden personal agendas—out of the discussion and minimize the risk of inappropriate outbursts. It's not always pleasant playing referee, but sometimes it's unavoidable.

CHAPTER 7

HANDLING THE TOUGH ONES:

*Dealing with
Difficult
Situations*

"Curiouser and curiouser," cried Alice.

—*Alice's Adventures in Wonderland*

No one promised running a meeting would be a piece of cake, and from time to time you are bound to encounter tough situations and difficult people. Participants who won't stop talking, people who have nothing to say and spend hours saying it, angry people and stubborn people, squabblers and tyrants—these are some of the characters you're likely to encounter. Then there are the meetings that won't fly, and the black holes. With a little practice, however, you'll learn to negotiate your way through even the toughest of challenges. There are a couple of general rules that can and should be applied to all the challenges you are likely to run up against.

All Problems Are "People" Problems; Approach Them From That Perspective. A blown fuse on the slide projector is easily remedied: just replace the fuse. But, except for a mechanical breakdown, the problems that affect meetings are caused by people, and you can't simply throw out the problem and start over. People problems are driven by egos, insecurities, ambitions, moods, likes and dislikes, and personalities. However unproductive that blowhard across the room is, the one who has monopolized the conversation with irrelevant remarks, telling him to put a sock in it may only create a new problem. Bearing this in mind will help you find the appropriate solution without creating new difficulties.

Keep Personalities and Value Judgments Out of the Solution. In moments of frustration, it is often tempting to offer assumptions, evaluations, or opinions as the reason for someone else's shortcoming: "If you didn't waste so much time, you would have finished that assignment," or, "If you weren't so stubborn, you'd see the other side of the question." In resolving problems during a meeting, keep personalities out of the solution. Deal with the problem; forgo your opinions about why it exists, however right they may be. There is no place for embarrassment or humiliation in the work environment, and personal comments are at best unproductive, because they further alienate the recipient. Stick to the facts: If the work was not done, what can be done to resolve that problem? or, a particular individual is unable, or unwilling, to see both sides of an issue; what can be done to help him see differently?

In an article entitled "When Your Attendees Turn Ugly" (*Meetings & Conventions,* May 1988), psychologist Marion Jacobs of UCLA urges meeting planners to stick to the facts and avoid acting defensively. "Show him that you're not going to fight with him. Once he sees that, you defuse all the tension," she says.

HANDLING DIFFICULT SITUATIONS

The first question to be answered in finding solutions to difficult situations is, "When is a problem a problem?" The answer is simple:

> *A problem is any action or condition that serves to prevent you, as meeting leader, from accomplishing your purpose.*

Distraction, delay, obstacle, inertia, boredom, inappropriate emotions—any of these can be a problem if it prevents the meeting from moving forward.

What follows are some of the most common difficulties you are likely to encounter and some possible approaches to resolving them.

The Yakkers. These are the people who sit across the room and, heads together, carry on a whispered conversation while the rest of the group is either listening to a speaker or attempting to discuss an idea. Nothing is louder than a whisper in this situation; quickly heads turn, the speaker stumbles, and if not nipped in the bud, one whisper generates others and the meeting grinds to a halt.

One solution is to stop the meeting momentarily to let the whisperers finish their conversation or at least get the message that you would appreciate their silence. A glance in their direction might also serve the purpose; as last resort, you might ask one of the culprits if he or she has anything to add to what is being discussed.

The Interminables. These are the well-intentioned people who, though they have many ideas to contribute, tend to go on and on and on without any organization to their thoughts and with a great deal of repetition.

Look for an appropriate moment to politely break into these monologues. Thank the speaker for his or her ideas, recognize their value, and then shift the focus to someone else. "George, I wonder if I might interrupt for a moment. I'm interested in that idea, and I wonder if anyone else has a comment on it."

The Vacuums. From time to time you will encounter an individual who is firmly convinced that he or she has volumes to contribute, whereas in fact his or her comments are irrelevant to any discussion and serve only to shift the focus away from the work to be done.

At first you might try guiding such people back to the subject with questions. If this does not work, and it probably won't, the only solution may be to ignore them as politely as possible. This can be done by calling on other speakers and, seemingly accidentally, overlooking their requests to talk.

The Squabblers. These are the fighters, those unhappy individuals who need to take on the world, sometimes quite offensively. In a meeting situation they disagree with every idea proposed and belittle other participants. There is simply no room in a meeting for this kind of behavior.

First of all, be aware that such an individual is using the meeting situation to express fears and emotions that have nothing to do with the present situation. There is no use confronting such an individual about emotions. Questions about anger or abusiveness will only be met with denial.

You may try to rally group consensus against the squabbler's approach in the hope that prevailing odds will quiet him. "George thinks we are wasting our time, that this is a ridiculous idea. Do the rest of you agree?" It is also perfectly appropriate to ask the individual to stop the behavior. Do so directly and calmly, without adding any personal opinion about his character. "George, I think those kinds of comments are preventing us from accomplishing what we've set out to do. I would appreciate it if you would refrain from making them." If all else fails, ask him to leave the meeting and suggest a private conference with you later in the day.

The Mules. Few people are more exasperating than the individual who clings to an idea and argues for it relentlessly. Long after the topic of conversation has changed, there she is, raising her pet issue again and again. She slows the progress of the meeting, delays decisions, and serves as a thorn in the side of other participants.

When it becomes obvious that this is a person with a mission, let her state her case and then politely avoid her. If she succeeds in raising the topic once again, find the opportunity to settle the matter by involving the rest of the group. Thank her for her idea and ask several others for contrasting views. If she persists, put the matter to a vote. "Mary feels strongly that this is the best way to go on this project. I'd like to see a show of hands of those who agree with her."

The Tyrants. Tyrants are those characters who have an opinion about everything. They never shut up. Whatever the subject, they're experts. Their effect on a meeting is like that of chlorine in a swimming pool: They kill every sign of life.

Once again, politely ignoring that waving, frantic hand may help some. But tyrants may have valuable contributions to make, however offensively they make them. Try to keep their comments as brief as possible. Find a moment to interrupt, recognize what has been said by rephrasing it or summarizing the main points, and then let the group know that you would like its involvement as well: "George, that's an interesting viewpoint, but I'd really like to hear some others. Would anyone else care to comment?" The key to taming The Tyrant is matching their output with other speakers.

The Lost Souls. The meeting has been underway for forty-five minutes, and in wanders The Lost Soul. "Sorry I'm late," she says, and then does one of two things: "Where are we," she asks. "Can someone bring me up to date?" or else she proceeds to jump into the conversation, eloquently arguing points that have been discussed long before she arrived. At best The Lost Soul is a distraction, throwing the conversation momentarily into reverse.

Deal with this one quickly by saying, "I'll fill you in at the break, Mary." Draw her attention to the printed agenda and whatever background or collateral materials have been distributed and suggest, "Take a look through those while we finish up this topic."

The Bosses. This can be the deadliest situation of all. Your meeting is in full swing. Ideas are flying, the enthusiasm is high when in walks The Boss. A second later she says, "I know you are the experts in this matter, but it seems to me the best idea would be . . ." Suddenly, the enthusiasm is gone; the ideas have vanished. Who can argue with The Boss? Now there is more concern about looking good and sounding smart than throwing ideas against the wall.

What to do? Throw her out? Hardly. But you can be firm, and you can trust your own judgment. Don't hesitate to reinforce the contributions already made by the group members: "Before you came in, we came up with some ideas that I think are worth considering." Give credit to individuals for their contributions to the meeting. Keep control of the meeting; she may be The Boss, but it's your show. Respond to her comments by asking for other ideas *without* asking the other participants to comment on the boss's contribution.

The Silence. Much like a Stephen King horror novel, this situation can strike terror in the heart of a meeting leader. You bounce into the meeting, enthusiasm at a peak, throw out the first few questions or topics, and what happens? Nothing. The room is silent. Eyes stare at note pads, throats are cleared, feet shuffle, and no one says a word.

What can you do? First of all, try to determine the problem. Is the group prepared? Do the participants need more information? Is it clear what you're asking for? Have you somehow cowed them? Then start again: "Let's backtrack a minute, because I'd like you all to understand what we have to do here today." Begin with the agenda, making clear what you intend to discuss. Ask if everyone received the background materials and if there are any questions. Finally, you do the talking for a while. Give the group the chance to size you up and get a feel for your style and your expectations. Then single out specific individuals to answer questions rather than throwing the question to the group as a whole.

The Wall. This is the moment when everything grinds to a halt; the group is deadlocked and going in circles. The same arguments are raised and refuted again and again. The Wall is a waste of time and needs to be broken down quickly.

Take charge by summarizing the arguments or ideas for the group. Don't ask for clarification or agreement, and then put the matter to a vote. Conclude the proceedings: "I think we've covered the subject pretty well. As I understand it, these are our options. The time has come to decide. How many are in favor of . . ." If the situation does not call for a vote, perhaps the issue can be left with a summary and a further assignment: "This is the way I see our discussion. By next week I'd like each of you to come up with three solutions to the problem." The key to breaking down The Wall is shifting the process from discussion to action.

If all efforts to break a deadlock fail, it may be advisable to end the meeting and schedule another, preferably with a different cast of characters, so that the same deadlock is not repeated.

The Black Hole. The Black Hole is a case of terminal boredom. The crowd is listless, restless, and unproductive. Whispered conversations break out across the room, bodies slip out to the restrooms, papers rustle, and faces stare blankly at the ceiling. Not an atmosphere conducive to accomplishing your goal.

Make a quick mental review of the situation. Have you exhausted the topic? Are you not making yourself clear? Do you need a break? Do you need to lighten up? Whatever the problem, the first step, in most cases, is a break. If more work must be accomplished, first give everyone a chance to shift gears, refresh themselves, maybe even go out of the room and gripe about your handling of the meeting. When the meeting resumes, restate the group's position with respect to the subject under discussion. Help the players to make a per-

sonal connection to the subject. Be sure that they understand its significance in relation to the company's larger
operations and help them see where their individual role
fits in.

THE STAFF MEETING

Probably the most common of all business meetings, staff
meetings are often the deadliest as well. You'd think, with
all the practice, that we'd have gotten it right by now. In
fact, staff meetings are too often boring and unproductive.
Why?

The most likely reason is that staff meetings are usually taken for granted, by the participants as well as the
leader. Because most happen routinely and according to
company policy, they are often poorly prepared and without purpose.

If your company policy calls for regular staff meetings
whether they are needed or not, the least you can do is
make it productive. Be sure that the meeting each week
has a stated purpose that requires some kind of action.
It's not enough to say, "Okay, let's hear what you guys
have been doing. Fine, good-bye." At the end of each
meeting, hand out assignments: "George, by next week
I want you to have done — — — and be ready to report on
the results."

Keep staff meetings short; there's no reason why the
department's business cannot be taken care of in half an
hour. Add some variety: change the meeting's location, if
possible, or surprise the group with different refreshments each week. Most of all, use the opportunity of a
staff meeting to reward and encourage as well as make
assignments: "I'm very pleased with the work you did
on — — —, George. Congratulations," or, "Kathy, your
writing is coming along very well. If you need more help,
let me know." With very little effort on your part, the
deadly staff meeting can become an important motivational
tool, as well as a communications device.

When dealing with difficult situations, learn from your experience. After each meeting, take time to review the problem areas.

- What was my role?
- What did I do right?
- What could I have done differently?
- What are my strengths and weaknesses in handling that particular situation?

Answer those questions, jot down your answers for safekeeping, and you'll find that handling difficult people and tough situations will soon become a manageable, even challenging part of running a productive meeting.

CHAPTER 8

COLLATERAL MATERIALS:

Reinforcement Rather than Distraction

The Fish-Footman began by producing from under his arm a great letter, nearly as large as himself.

—*Alice's Adventures in Wonderland*

A dozen people sit around a large conference table. In front of each person is a stack of papers, charts, and reports. Some are reading, some have dropped their materials on the floor, one holds a chart up to the light, and still others are rustling through their stacks. The leader of the meeting is making a presentation, but is soon interrupted with, "Excuse me, where are we in this report?" What's wrong here? A valuable meeting tool is being misused.

Collateral materials or handouts can be a fine addition to a meeting, but all too often they serve merely to distract and to slow the proceedings. As a meeting leader, one of your important tasks is learning how and when to use printed materials to increase the productivity of your meeting.

There is a simple rule to follow:

Collateral materials should provide necessary information, clarify a discussion, or reinforce a point; they should never become the subject of the meeting.

Good collateral materials are relevant to the subject being discussed and are easily understood without disrupting the flow of conversation.

What are collateral materials? Collaterals are any kind of printed matter that is given to participants before, during, or after a meeting. A printed agenda, workbooks or worksheets, questionnaires and surveys, charts, written reports, statistics, news clips, marketing or sales plans, speeches, proposals, press kits and press releases—these can all be collateral material.

The first question to answer is whether to use collateral materials. The answer is yes, if you need to; no, if you plan to use them as a substitute for adequate preparation; yes, if they will lend support to your ideas or position; no, if they will distract your colleagues from what you have to say.

If you feel that reinforcement is necessary, there are several rules that, if followed, will help you make collaterals a valuable addition to your meeting.

1. Allow Plenty of Time for Planning

It takes time to prepare printed materials. They must be written, often designed, printed, and distributed. Be sure you coordinate your plans with everyone involved in the preparation process—writers, designers, editors, printers, mailroom staff—so that no link is missing. Also, let the meeting participants know what materials you plan to distribute so that duplication is avoided and everyone knows what to expect. If you've decided to distribute the materials in advance of the meeting, be sure to allow enough time for delivery and reading. A useful tool is a written timetable detailing exactly when each piece of material will be completed, the date of distribution, and names of those people receiving the material.

2. Collaterals Should Be Written in Outline Form, Using As Few Words As Possible

This is especially true if they are to be used during the meeting. A simplified form minimizes the distribution factor by allowing participants to concentrate on what is being said instead of reading the material. Materials to be distributed after the meeting may cover the topic in greater detail.

3. If Thorough Reading of a Document Is Necessary to the Conduct of the Meeting, Be Sure That Participants Have It Well Before the Date of the Meeting

Do not read a document in its entirety during a meeting, no matter how important; it is a waste of everyone's time. You may assume that it has been read (if you distributed it in time) and simply summarize its contents during the meeting.

4. "Walking" the Group Through a Report or Presentation Is Ineffective and Often Irritating

A common practice, "walking" your audience through a document means leading it, page by page, through a report of some kind. Too often this technique masks a lack of preparation or lack of confidence on the part of the presenter. The process itself is distracting, as everyone fumbles with pages. If you want to make a written presentation, let the audience read it before joining the meeting; the meeting itself should be devoted to an oral presentation that is reinforced by the report.

5. Collateral Material Should Be the Subject of a Meeting Only If It Is the Subject of the Meeting

If you are presenting a new ad campaign to a client, it is understandable that photographs, printed material, slides, and videos will be the topic of discussion. But only in cases when the visual media are the message should printed materials be the focus of the meeting. Otherwise, collaterals should complement the oral presentation or discussion.

6. Make Use of Overhead Projectors and Other Audiovisual Equipment to Minimize the Use of Printed Materials

Charts, graphs, and statistics may be vital to the conduct of your meeting. If so, it may be better to display them through use of audiovisual devices than to distribute a printout to each participant during the meeting. This minimizes the distraction factor and helps focus the attention of the entire group.

7. When Possible, Distribute Collateral Materials After the Meeting

There may be occasions when you need to give out materials for use during the meeting. (The agenda is one item that must always be handed out as the meeting starts.) In general, however, hand out materials during the meeting only if they are essential to the conduct of business or if they significantly enhance your position. If, on the other hand, they are repetitions or summaries of the oral presentation or discussion, they are best given out after meeting so they do not serve as a distraction.

8. Material Prepared for Background Should Be Clearly and Comprehensively Written

Any documents prepared to be distributed before or after a meeting—reports, speeches, press kits or releases, proposals—should cover all the major elements of the topic in a self-explanatory fashion. Remember, the reader will not be able to ask you questions. The material should follow the sequence in which the topic is discussed in the meeting, and only relevant information should be included.

9. As Meeting Leader, Maintain Control of What Materials Will Be Handed Out

Be sure that you discuss with all other meeting participants what materials are to be distributed. This helps you set the tone for the meeting and enables you to eliminate any materials that are counterproductive to your goals.

CHAPTER 9

AUDIOVISUAL ASSISTANCE:

Enhancement Rather than Clutter

*Take care of the sense, and the sounds
will take care of themselves.*

—*Alice's Adventures in Wonderland*

At a recent monthly meeting of a local Kiwanis Club, an area businessman was invited to talk about the challenge of keeping a major grocery store stocked with fresh fish, fruit, and vegetables. The speaker was a kindly sort who was well known in the community for his warmth and sense of humor.

The businessman had brought his slides with him, and his talk began with shots of a large truck on its way to the Boston markets in the wee hours of the morning. As he warmed up to the subject, the slides came faster and faster. And then one appeared upside down, and his listeners tilted their heads to look at a swordfish from Vietnam. Then there was a picture of the businessman's grandchildren, and he digressed a moment to discuss their schooling and latest feats of bravery and then went on back to vegetables. The presentation went on in this fashion—the occasional slide aslant or reversed, more shots of the kids, a few of his trip to Europe—and a good time was had by all.

This example illustrates the basic rule for using audiovisual elements in a meeting: Whatever you use should enhance the presentation and not distract from it. Slides of your grandchildren or grandparents and shots of the family vacation are certainly inappropriate in most business meetings but, intentionally or otherwise, in a less formal setting such as the local Kiwanis meeting they served to create an image for the speaker—that of a generous, friendly soul who, by the way, is one hell of a businessman as well.

Properly used in a meeting, visuals can accomplish many things. They can reinforce the key points of a presentation; lend an air of glamor or style to a meeting; generate a specific image or tone; and enhance understanding, help convince the viewer, and move the presentation along by dividing it into highly visible units or sections. Visuals can also help speakers organize their thoughts and structure their presentation.

On the other hand, visuals can be distracting and confusing and can create a false or misguided impression or image for you or your company. To be effective, visuals should always play a supporting role, reinforcing your position, ideas, or goals; they should never overshadow or distort them.

The variety of visual aids available for use in meetings is staggering. There are slides, films, videos, television shows, audio presentations, overhead projections, blackboards, easels, charts, photographs, and three-dimensional displays. The latest, of course, is computer graphics and software. Your choice will depend on several factors: the atmosphere you wish to create, the type of meeting you have planned, and how you intend to use audiovisuals to supplement your presentation.

For a briefing in which one or more speakers will stand before an audience, you may decide on a slide presentation, film or video. For a roundtable working session, an overhead projector may be more suitable. For a sales presentation or new business pitch, you may combine video, computers, slides, charts, and photo displays. For a training session, you may need only charts and graphs.

Each piece of equipment or concept has its own strengths and weaknesses. The overhead projector, for example, has wonderful versatility. You can display charts, graphs, drawings, and documents in black and white or color. You can write and draw on the transparencies as you go along. You can even do overlays by piling one transparency on top of another. A 1981 study commissioned by the 3M Company and executed by the Wharton School of Business at the University of Pennsylvania found that meetings in which overhead transparencies are used are shorter and that the presenter is perceived to be better prepared.

The disadvantage of overheads is they are only as impressive as the presenter's use of them and that, with the recent explosion in computer software, they may seem dated in certain situations. For example, an engineering firm in New York recently created a state-of-the-art, three-dimensional computer model to bid on the contract to rebuild a major part of the city's subway system. Flip charts or overhead transparencies in that situation would have been less impressive.

The use of audiovisuals in a meeting requires a three-step process: organization, preparation, and implementation.

1. Organization

To organize the audiovisual component of your meeting, first decide on your reason for including it in your presentation. Do you want to create a dazzling, forceful image or do you need a working tool to conduct a discussion? Is cost a factor? Does your budget restrict your use of expensive equipment or the preparation of slides, tapes, or displays?

Then list all the materials you will need and how long it will take to obtain or prepare them. Don't forget to allow enough time to prepare overhead transparencies, slides, or videos. If you plan to engage a professional to create your visuals, try to give him or her as much time as possible; the more time he or she has to work with, the less costly it will be. If you need something tomorrow, be prepared to pay for it.

2. Preparation

The preparation stage may be handled by your staff, an outside firm, or a combination of the two. Allow yourself enough time to collect all the information that will go on the transparencies or slides. It is sound business practice to create an audiovisual checklist, separate from your meeting preparation checklist, on which you include all material to be produced and a list of all equipment to be used. Be sure that each deadline is met and confirmed.

3. Implementation

Implementing the audiovisual component of the meeting, of course, depends on what equipment you have chosen to use. Be certain, before the meeting, that the room to be used is equipped properly and that the seating is arranged so that all participants can see the visuals. Make sure that the equipment is near enough to an electrical outlet so that you don't have to reorganize the room after everyone has arrived. If you are meeting in a hotel or someone else's office, be sure you know whom to contact in case of technical failure. Finally, don't try to do everything yourself. It is often most convenient for the speaker to use a remote when using a slide projector during a presentation, but you shouldn't have to run back and forth between VCR and podium or attempt to manipulate an overhead projector if the task simply involves changing transparencies. If you do use an assistant, have a rehearsal; be certain that the assistant is familiar with the equipment and its use as well as with the sequence of materials to be shown. The assistant also should be familiar with your presentation so that you don't have to pause repeatedly to call out for a new picture.

Always bear in mind the old saying, "A picture is worth a thousand words." Like it or not, you will be judged by the audiovisuals you choose. Even your choice of colors will have an impact. Be certain that they, and all your visuals, convey an image that is appropriate to the event, the company, and you. This is why corporations spend millions developing a logo, why the advertising industry is alive and well, and why image consultants get paid big bucks. It is nice to believe that intelligence, expertise, and the ability to communicate are the qualities by which we are perceived, but the fact is that, if an impression has to be made quickly (as in a meeting), a visual impression has the most impact. For that reason, as you consider the use of visuals in your next meeting, remember that no visual impact at all may be more productive than an ill-conceived one.

CHAPTER 10 WRAPPING
IT UP:

*When is
Enough
Enough?*

"I shall sit here," the Footman remarked, "till tomorrow—or the next day, maybe."

—*Alice's Adventures in Wonderland*

"It ain't over till it's over." Truer words were never spoken when it comes to meetings. There are two kinds of meeting time: agenda time—the hours and minutes *scheduled* for the meeting—and real time—how long the meeting actually takes. If you do your job as meeting leader properly, *real time should never be longer than agenda time.* And it never hurts if it's a bit shorter.

Like a good book, a well-run meeting has a structure. There is a beginning, a middle, and an end. Why is the end of the meeting important? Why not wait for the bell to ring, slam the book shut in midsentence, and walk out?

The first reason is courtesy: The participants, who have committed their time and energy to work with you, deserve better than rudeness. There are certain formalities that are expected and appreciated in the course of human interaction, one of which is finishing properly what you've started.

The end of a meeting is more than a formality, however. It includes important business and sets the stage for the next phase of action.

There really is no *one* end to a meeting. Rather, there is a series of endings that culminates in the final wrap-up. As discussed in previous chapters, the meeting process involves several stages: information is presented; then it is discussed; decisions are made; and, finally, actions are agreed on. Each of these stages must be ended properly before moving on to the next. Further, depending on the content of the meeting, each stage may include substages that must also be finished before the meeting moves on. For example, if the meeting involves the presentation and discussion of several topics, each one must be introduced and analyzed in an orderly fashion. For the meeting leader, this requires the skillful opening and closing of many discussions. These "mini-endings," as we will see, are simply minor variations on the process of ending the meeting.

In the dictionary, the word "conclusion" has several related meanings: the end of something, the outcome or result of a process, a judgment or decision reached after deliberation, a final settlement, and the closing of a discourse that contains a summing up. This, then, is what you are doing when you end a meeting: The meeting is concluded.

Concluding a meeting is a three-step process: preparing the group for the conclusion, wrapping up the findings and decisions, and expressing appreciation for the work accomplished.

1. Preparing to Conclude the Meeting

The meeting leader is in many ways like a director of a play: He or she is the only participant who has an overall view, a perspective on the entire stage. The other players have their individual interests and preoccupations; the leader watches out for the group. For this reason, it is necessary to prepare the meeting participants for the end of the session.

You can do this simply by saying, ten minutes before the meeting is over, "Let's wrap it up, folks; we have to be out of here in a few minutes." This gives the participants time to organize their thoughts, have a last word, and mentally sum up for themselves what the meeting has meant. It starts them thinking about the next step—what actions they need to take from this point on.

2. Wrapping It Up

Wrapping up a meeting means summarizing the proceedings for the group, including repeating the meeting's purpose, and then outlining what happened. Be sure to summarize what was discussed, what decisions were made and what, if anything, was *not* accomplished. You should also emphasize what actions will be taken on the basis of the decisions made, who will take those actions, and when the work is expected to be completed.

Here's an example: "As you know, our purpose today was to come up with a plan to market our new client, Fred Foiegras, who believes he can become rich and famous by sticking his head in a bucket and making motorboat noises" (this was actually seen on *The Tonight Show*; names have been changed here to protect the ridiculous).

"We analyzed the results of a market study, discussed several promotional ideas and concluded that a) the best route to take is a major market media tour in which we place Mr. Foiegras on TV talk shows, and b) we get our money up front. The next step will be to develop a media tour plan, which will be supervised by George. I'd like to see a draft of that in two weeks. In the next few days, I will meet with the client to determine if he has any other skills—such as motorcycle noises that might strengthen our campaign" (he did).

3. Expressing Appreciation

In concluding the meeting, be sure to thank the participants. This should include a collective thank-you to the group and recognition of individual contributions that were significant to the success of the meeting. Many meeting leaders make the mistake of limiting their words of appreciation to "Thanks for coming today." The fact is that most of those in attendance probably had no choice in the matter; they were there because they were compelled in one way or another. A more appropriate expression of appreciation might be, "Thank you for your contributions and the time you've taken to think about what we've discussed. Your help has been appreciated."

When should you end a meeting? The answer is: when the work has been accomplished or the allotted time for the meeting is up, whichever comes first. You should never carry a meeting past its announced conclusion time, because other participants have tight schedules and commitments in other places. They have met their half of the bargain by agreeing to your announced time frame; it's your responsibility to meet your half by sticking to it. If there's a crisis — a situation in which work has to be completed immediately regardless of how long it takes — all participants should be notified of this *in advance* of the meeting so that they can be prepared to stay indefinitely.

It is advisable to end a meeting before its scheduled conclusion if your purpose has been accomplished *or* if the proceedings are hopelessly bogged down. If your discussion seems to be going in circles and nothing you try to get it back on track is working, then it's time to stop for the day and reschedule.

CHAPTER 11

THUMBS UP OR DOWN:

*Assessing
the Meeting*

"If there's no meaning in it," said the
King, *"that saves a world of trouble,
you know, as we needn't try to find
any."*

—*Alice's Adventures in Wonderland*

Most of us go through life placing values on our impressions and experiences: "What a beauty!" "That was a great meal!" "I loved that movie!" We evaluate, according to our own standards and tastes, what we see, feel, hear, or taste. Why? Why not just say, "That was a meal," or "That was a movie"? Or, "That was a meeting." There are several reasons.

An evaluation makes something complete. It helps us to shape and give meaning to an experience, and this, in turn, allows us to place that experience in perspective. The human animal needs to create an order in which to live; chaos doesn't work. To evaluate something is to give order to it and to our relationship to it.

Assessing or evaluating a meeting allows us to say, "Yes, I understand what this means. I know what importance it has. I know what to do with it. I know the next step to take." Without such an assessment, a meeting is an experience without value to its participants. Without an assessment there is no way to determine whether the meeting's purpose was achieved, thus making the meeting purposeless.

In the simplest terms the meeting assessment answers three questions:

- What happened?
- What was accomplished?
- What was not accomplished?

By answering those questions, you are able to organize your thoughts, understand the significance of the decisions made at the meeting, plan the next step, and identify areas of possible improvement in your skills.

The core of an assessment is the summary of the proceedings you make at the conclusion of the meeting. This summary outlines the facts and ideas introduced and the decisions made at the meeting. The next step is to place a value on these and other actions — to rate the meeting. The most efficient way to assess a meeting is by using a checklist for your personal reference. Remember that while elements of your assessment will be incorporated into a final, public report on the meeting, the checklist is essentially for your confidential use. It is a tool for self-improvement.

The checklist that follows is intended only as a guide; you may require fewer or more entries, depending on the specifics of your meeting. Most, but not all, questions can be answered *yes* or *no*. In determining how you might have handled the meeting differently, be sure to be specific and comprehensive.

MEETING ASSESSMENT CHECKLIST

Meeting Purpose or Objective

Was it designed to generate concrete results (decisions, actions)?
Was the accomplishment of the purpose measurable?
Was the purpose or objective achievable (realistic)?
How could I have structured the objective differently?

Participants

Were the right number of people invited?
Was the selection of the participants successful?
How could I have improved the participant list?

Preparations

Were invitations extended on time?
Were invitations followed up?
Was my own preparation of materials adequate?
Were participants prepared to discuss the topics of the meeting?
Were facilities and equipment arranged in time?
Were supplies adequate?
How could I have prepared for the meeting differently?

Quality of Discussion

Was there adequate discussion of topics?
Was group participation adequate?
Were all topics discussed?
Was enough time allotted for discussion?
How could I have managed the discussion phase of the meeting differently?

Decision Making

Were decisions made at the meeting?
Did the decisions help accomplish the purpose of the meeting?
Was there enough time to make all the decisions required?
Was the information provided in the meeting adequate for making decisions?

How could I have handled the decision making phase of the meeting differently?

Assignments

Were assignments for future action made on the basis of the decisions?

Did the assignments help accomplish the purpose of the meeting?

Did all participants leave the meeting with a clear understanding of their next task?

Is there a system in place to ensure that appropriate follow-ups will be made on actions to be taken?

How could I have made assignments differently?

Collaterals

Did collateral materials reinforce the subject(s) of the meeting?

Were the collaterals easily digested without being distracting to participants?

Were collaterals distributed at the right time?

How could the collaterals have been different?

Audiovisuals

Did the audiovisuals enhance the presentation?

Did they appropriately reflect the image of the company or speaker?

Should there have been more (or fewer) visuals?

Could audiovisuals have been used differently?

Timing

Did the meeting start on time?

Were all participants on time?

Did the meeting end on time?

Was there adequate time for the meeting?

How could I have structured the time element of the meeting differently?

Handling Problems

What problems were encountered during the meeting?

Were the problems adequately resolved?

How could I have handled the problems differently?

CHAPTER 12

WRITING IT UP:

*Reporting
the Results*

"Take pen and ink, and write it down."

—Alice's Adventures in Wonderland

If the opera isn't over until the fat lady sings, a meeting isn't over until you've written it up. By the end of a few strenuous hours in a conference room, the last thing you may want to do is give the meeting more thought, but a clearly written report of the proceedings will be an invaluable tool for several reasons, and you should be sure to make the effort.

THE PURPOSE OF THE FINAL REPORT

The final report on a meeting is a synopsis of the proceedings, including whatever decisions and actions were agreed on. Depending on the nature of the meeting, other follow-up materials may have to be prepared, such as research papers, surveys, market studies, proposals, and presentations, but the one document that must be completed for every meeting is the final report.

The final report accomplishes several things:

1. It Provides a Written Record of the Meeting's Proceedings

The human memory is an often unreliable tool; a document that describes the proceedings, although it certainly does not present a total, completely objective picture, at least provides a source to which people can refer for information, a record that, once written, does not change. (Some companies tape-record meetings in order to preserve a verbatim account of the proceedings. This would appear to be an extreme measure unless you are dealing with sensitive legal matters or you work in the Oval Office. But look what tapes did for Richard Nixon!)

2. The Final Report Makes Follow-Up Easier

A well-run meeting concludes with the assignment of further actions. A written report helps you and others remember to carry out those tasks and reinforces a sense of responsibility for those assignments. The report also serves to clarify the assignments, distinguishing between long-term and short-term projects, and provides participants a timetable to work with.

3. The Report Reminds All Participants of the Content of the Meeting, Any Decisions Made and Their Significance to Each Individual's Work

By reinforcing the ideas discussed during the meeting, the report keeps those ideas alive and stimulates their further consideration.

In summary, the final report puts into writing everything you concluded in the meeting and provides a vision of what happened and what must happen in the future. Because it is in writing and readily accessible, it acts as a reinforcement to your goals and helps you accomplish them.

THE FORM OF THE FINAL REPORT

Unless you have specific instructions to the contrary, the final report should be an elaboration of the minutes of the meeting. Properly recorded, the minutes should outline the entire proceedings of the meeting. They should in-

A MEETING PREPARATION
WORKSHEET/CHECKLIST

Purpose of Meeting (in 25 words or less):

Place:

Date:

Time:

List of Participants   Date Invited   Date Confirmed

Materials for Meeting   Date Completed

To Do On Day of Meeting   Done

Check location
Check supplies and materials
Check catering
Telephone reminder to participants

Follow Up to Meeting	Date Due	Date Completed
Minutes of the meeting		
Follow-up telephone calls		
Follow-up reports (list)		
Final report/analysis		

Note: Depending on your position, the responsibility for ensuring that all the necessary preparations for the meeting are carried out may be yours or your assistant's. In either case, using a checklist is a good idea.

clude the ideas discussed (with contributions identified by participant) and decisions and assignments made, recording the proceedings in the order in which they took place.

The final report consists of the minutes (usually prepared by someone other than the meeting leader) plus your comments, observations, and corrections. The report should be as short as possible, in expanded outline form. You should avoid large blocks of dense copy; use short, declarative statements that express your thoughts in as few words as possible. Remember, you want the report to be read, not discarded; make it look appealing and quickly digestible.

Depending on the meeting, there may be more than one final report. As you conclude the meeting, you may need to ask for reports from other participants on specific aspects of the discussion. These documents should be included with or assimilated into your final report.

DISTRIBUTION OF THE FINAL REPORT

The distribution of the final report depends on the corporate structure of your company. Certainly your boss should get a copy, as should every participant. If the decisions made at the meeting might be of interest or help to other departments, the report should be sent to appropriate personnel in those departments. The report should be kept on file in case anyone else needs to see it.

The final report should be prepared and delivered as quickly as possible. If it is simply an expanded version of the minutes, it should be completed within three or four days. If there are other documents that will take time to prepare, send out the edited minutes of the meeting immediately with a note stating that the final report, with other papers, will follow shortly.

INDEX

Audiovisuals, 64–79
  implementing, 67–68
  organizing, 66
  preparing, 67
  success of, 79
  types of, 65

Black hole, the, 54–55
Boss, the, 11, 28, 52–53
Briefings, 14–15

Collateral materials, 58, 61,
  79
  audiovisual, 64–68, 79
  distribution of, 61
  preparing, 59, 61, 67
  types of, 60, 61
Communication:
  pointers for, 33–34
  between participants, 35,
  38
Conclusion of meeting, 70–73
  preparing for, 71
Cost:
  of meeting, 9–10, 20
  of participants' salaries,
  9–10

Discussions, 14–15, 78

Final report, 82–84
  distribution of, 84
  form of, 83–84
  purpose of, 82–83

Goals, 3
Group dynamics, 11, 43

Information:
  preparing, 21, 25, 29
  presenting, 29, 31–32
  providing, 9, 15, 24, 30
Meeting assessment check-
  list, 78–79
Meeting participants:
  conflicting opinions of, 45
  encouraging, 38–45
  expressing appreciation for,
  72–73
  getting the most from,
  43–44
  greeting, 39
  handling personality problems of, 48–55
  introducing, 31
  number of, 16–17
  personality types of, 50–55
  preparing, 24–26
  recognizing individual, 40
  respecting differences between, 39
  selecting, 15–16, 78
  verbal and nonverbal signs
  of, 41
Meeting preparation checklist, 85–86
Meetings:
  agenda of, 25, 30
  assessment of, 76–79
  audiovisuals for, see Audiovisuals
  briefing-type, 14-15
  bringing to a close, 70-73

Meetings (*cont.*):
  cost of, 9-10, 20
  discussion-type, 14-15, 78
  handling problems at,
      48-55, 79
  length of, 20-21
  location of, 19-20
  preparation for, 14-21, 25
  process of, 29-30
  seating plan for, 30-31
  scheduling, 10, 11, 17-19,
      32, 70, 79
  taking charge of, 28-36, 61
  types of, 14-15
Minutes, keeping, 36

Purpose of meeting, 2, 5, 8,
      15, 24, 78

accomplishing, 4, 11, 14,
      76-77
  formulating, 3, 4

Rules of meeting, 31

Silence, the, 53
Staff meetings, 55-56
Strategy of meetings, 29
Subject of meeting, 25, 44,
      60

Time restrictions:
  of collateral materials prep-
      aration, 59, 66
  of meeting, 32, 70-73, 79
  of options, 11
  of planning meeting, 10

The
Cassell
Business Success Guides
Series

Writing Effective Letters and Memos

0 304 34461 3

Winning with Difficult People

0 304 34460 5

Delegating Authority

0 304 34459 1

How to Negotiate a Bigger Raise

0 304 34458 3

Make Presentations with Confidence

0 304 34560 1

Running a Meeting that Works

0 304 34559 8